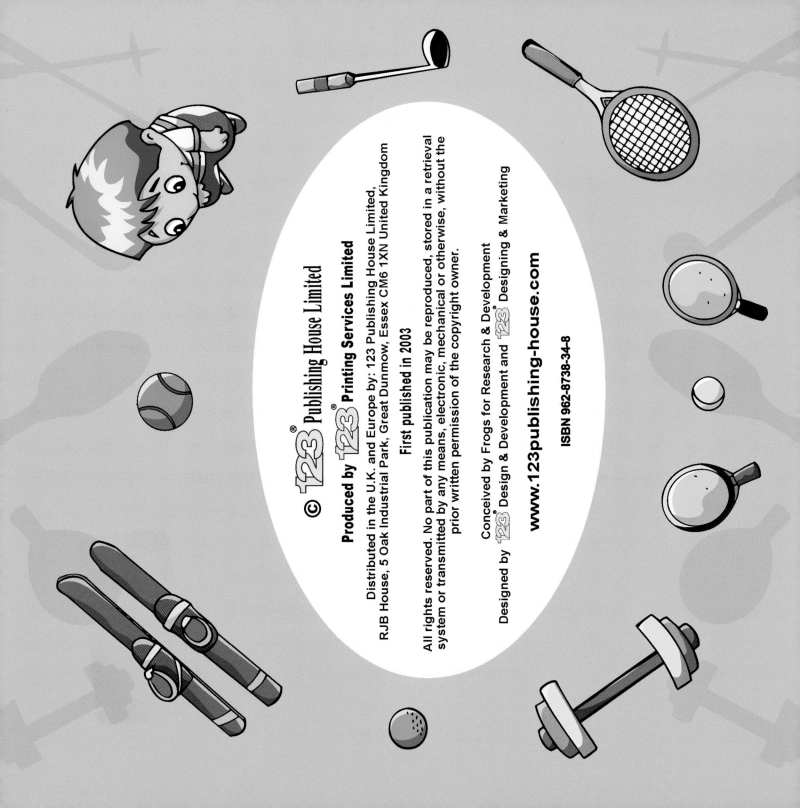

INDIVIDUAL SPORTS

123®

Weight lifting

Weight lifting makes your muscles stronger.

CHALK

chalk

weights

barbells

3

Golf

Golf is often played on courses with 18 holes.

golf bag

ball

golf club

flag

5

Skiing

Skiers slide down snow-covered hills on skis.

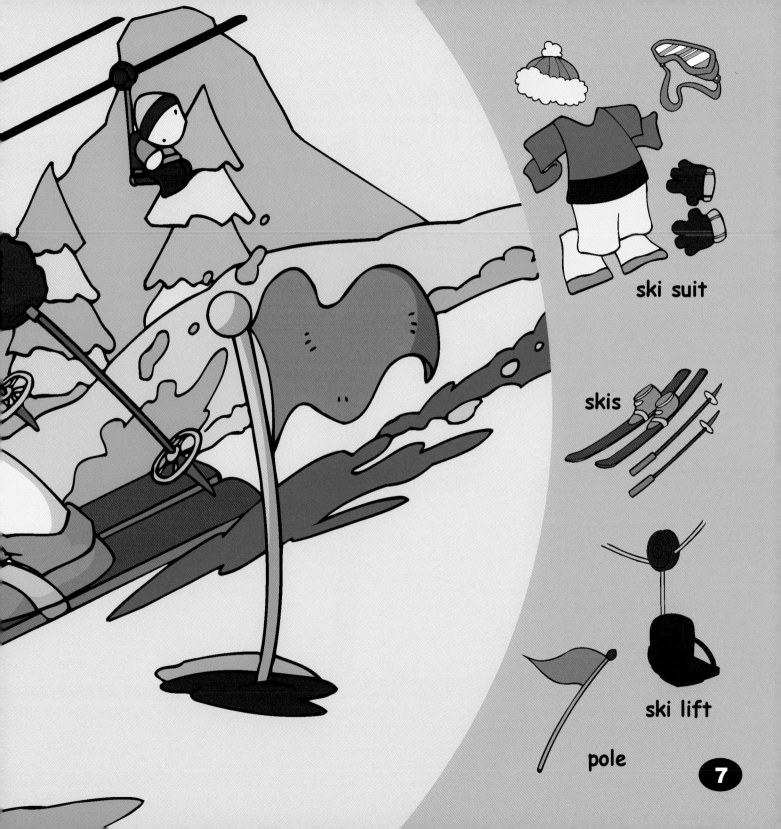

ski suit

skis

ski lift

pole

Gymnastics

You need to be very flexible to do gymnastics.

leotard

parallel bars

horse

mat

9

Shot put

Shotputters throw a heavy ball as far as they can.

shot

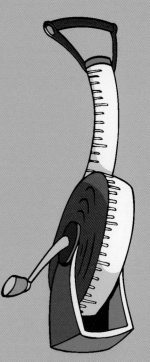

tape measure

Swimming

You swim in a swimming pool.

goggles

armband

swimming costume

swimming cap

Table tennis

Table tennis is played with a ping pong ball.

table tennis bat

ping pong ball

net

table

15

Horse riding

Horse riding requires good balance.

saddle

riding hat

boots

horse

17

Fencing

In fencing you fight against another person with a sword.

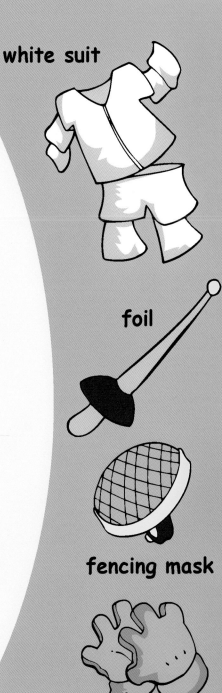

white suit

foil

fencing mask

gloves

19

Sprinting

Sprinters run very
fast for a short
distance.

vest

shorts

trainers

Tennis

You play tennis
with a racket.

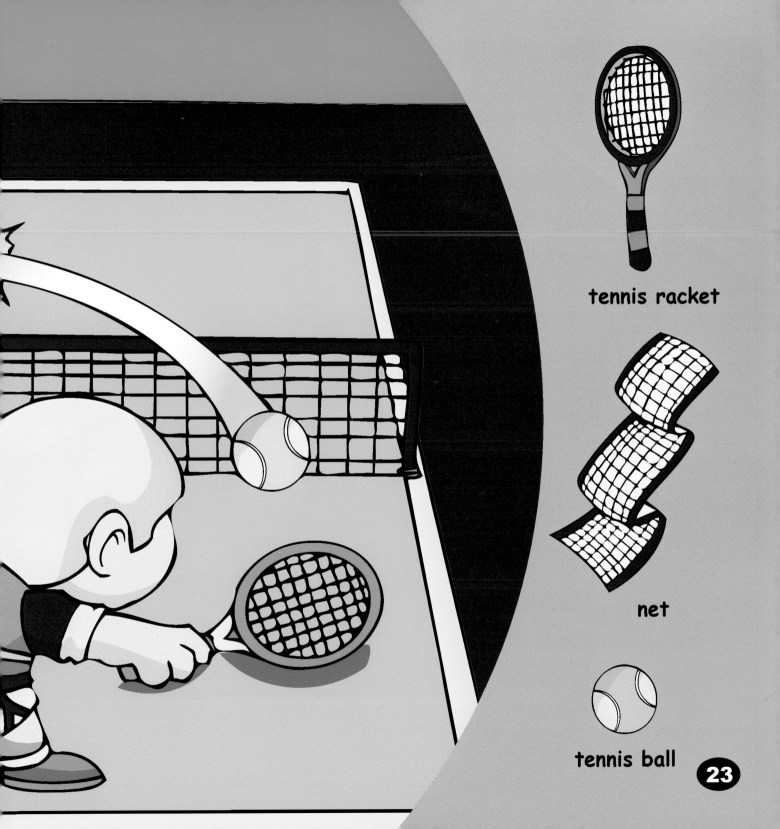

tennis racket

net

tennis ball

23

Trampolining

You bounce up and down
on a trampoline.

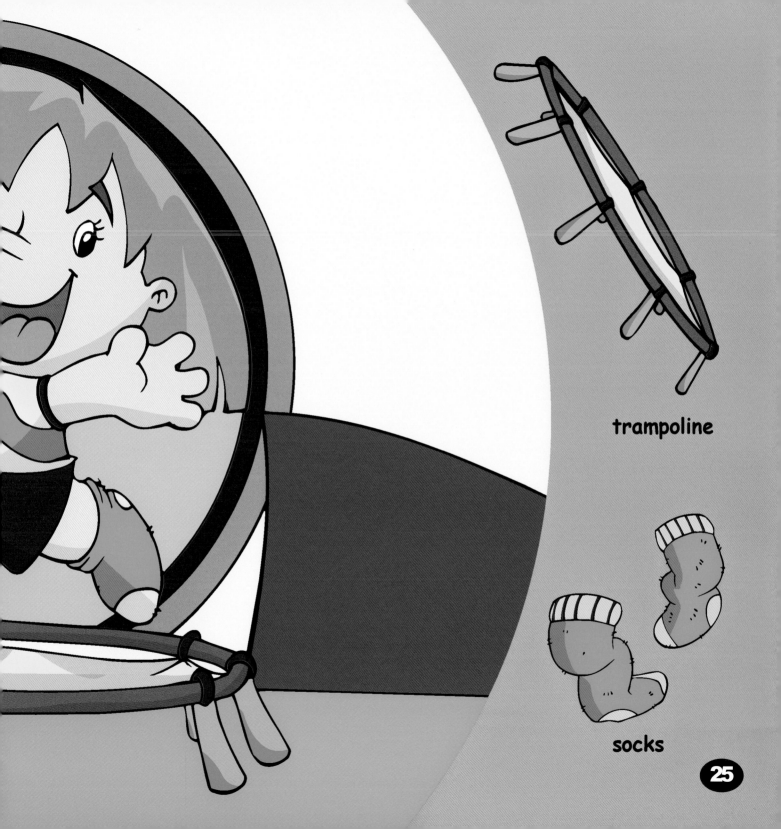

trampoline

socks

25